Rev. Dr. Richard Young

Above
and
Beyond

THE MYSTERY OF THE CROSS

CITIOFBOOKS, INC.
3736 Eubank NE Suite A1
Albuquerque, NM 87111-3579
www.citiofbooks.com
Hotline: 1 (877) 389-2759
Fax: 1 (505) 930-7244

Ordering Information:

Quantity sales. Special discounts are available on quantity purchases by corporations, associations, and others. For details, contact the publisher at the address above.

Printed in the United States of America.

ISBN-13:   Softcover   979-8-89391-217-3

                     Ebook   979-8-89391-218-0

Library of Congress Control Number: 2024914717

Above and Beyond
the
MYSTERY of the cross

Rev. Dr. Richard Young

CITI OF BOOKS

Table of Contents

Dedication

I want to dedicate this book to all the men and women of the world who teach and preach the word of our Lord and Savior Jesus Christ and to the mercy and grace of God.

I want to commend and give thanks to my wife, Linda Young, who has been much help to me and to the professors of E. K. Bailey Ministries.

Testimony of a Servant

I, Richard E. Young, a prisoner of Jesus Christ in July 9, 2010, I had a sudden attack of diverticulitis, that is bleeding from the intestines. Dr. McNair said, when he first looked at it, he thought it was cancer; he bowed his head and then he looked again and looked again, and saw it was not cancer. He sent me from his office to Ocean Springs Hospital; he did all he could to stop the bleeding and could not. They placed me in a room and gave me plazic to see if the bleeding would stop. It was late that evening. I tried to get up to go to the bathroom. I heard my wife say, "Not now, Lord," and screamed; that was the last thing I heard. I died in her arms, and in just a moment, I had passed from this life into the third heaven. I was facing westward and a supernatural creature came from beneath me on my left side and laid his hands on me and turn me northeast. I had no memory of the world which I had left, none at all. I just knew I was in a place I had never been before. I looked and saw a man standing afar off, then He turned and walked toward me and I said, "Oh my god." I saw Him walking in His glory and power, He turned into a light so bright I could not see, only the flashes of His glory! Then He took me within Himself and engulfed me; in just a moment, He brought me back and placed me back into my body. I could feel my life entering into my body. I opened my eyes and saw my wife, Linda, the children, and grandchildren, doctors, and nurses standing around the bed; it was then I knew from whence I had come from and that my eyes had seen the risen Christ. God has made me an eyewitness to the resurrection. When Dr. McNair received the report, he said, "Reverend, the Lord was with you." After getting out of the hospital, I went to the Tabernacle Baptist Church where Dr. McNair is a member and Dr. Kenneth Maurice Davis is the pastor; it was during this time that Dr. McNair asked me to pray for him because I had been with God. It is my hope that if accepted, that all men will seek to know the supreme power which is obtained by faith.

Introduction

I am most grateful and humble that God entrusted an ordinary man like me to share with the world the mystery of the cross, being saved by faith through grace and not by works, and to help believers, both ministers and laypersons, in their understanding, the unadulterated gospel of Jesus, the preaching and teaching of God's word. It is my hope and prayers that the inspired word of God will lead men, women, boys, and girls to give their hearts and lives to Christ and to secure the eternal life that is offered.

The cross is a demonstration to us in Christ Jesus, our Lord; in whom we have redemption through His blood, the forgiveness of sin, according to the riches of His grace.

Out of the mercy and grace of God, His word has flowed; let every person know that God will have mercy upon him, forgiving and using him to fulfill His glorious plan of salvation.

For God so loved the world, that He gave His only begotten Son, that whosoever believeth in Him should not perish, but have everlasting life. For God sent not His son into the world to condemn the world, but that the world through Him might be saved.

For this is good and acceptable in the sight of God our Savior: who will have all men to be saved, and to come unto the knowledge of the truth.

The Mystery of the Cross

This story was foretold centuries ago by the prophet Isaiah, Isaiah prophecy is found in Isaiah 53:1—10.

Verse 1: Who hath believed our report? And to whom is the arm of the Lord revealed?

Verse 2: For he shall grow up before him as a tender plant, and as a root out of a dry ground: he hath no form nor comeliness; and when we shall see him, there is no beauty that we should desire him.

Verse 3: He is despised and rejected of men, a man of sorrows, and acquainted with grief: and we hid as it were our faces from him; he was despised, and we esteemed him not.

Verse 4: Surely he hath borne our griefs, and carried our sorrows: yet we did esteem him stricken, smitten of God, and afflicted.

Verse 5: but he was wounded for our transgression; he was bruised for our iniquities: the chastisement of our peace was upon him; and with his stripes we are healed.

Verse 6: All we like sheep have gone astray; we have turned everyone to his own way; and the Lord hath laid on him the iniquity of us all.

Verse 7: He was oppressed, and he was afflicted, yet he opened not his mouth; he is brought as a lamb to the slaughter, and as a sheep before her shearers is dumb, so he opened not his mouth.

Verse 8: He was taken from prison and from judgment; and who shall declare his generation? For he was cut off

out of the land of the living: for the transgression of
my people was he stricken.

Verse 9: And he made his grave with the wicked and with the
rich in his death; because he had done no violence,
neither was any deceit in his mouth.

Verse 10: Yet it pleased the Lord to bruise him; he hath put
him to grief: when thou shalt make his soul an
offering for sin, he shall see his seed, he shall prolong
his days, and the pleasure of the Lord shall prosper
in his hand.

And now let us take a look at the picture that the Prophet Isaiah
talked about in the Old Testament. Now in the New Testament, the
account of the cross was recorded by Matthew 27 and Luke 23.

There has been difference of opinions for centuries even since the
crucifixion; theologians have debated whether the thief was saved or
not. I have personally pursued this mystery for many years, and then
one day, the whole thing open up by divine revelation, and that which
has been hidden came to life.

The Apostle Paul said it in 1 Corinthians 2:7-10.

Verse 7: But we speak the wisdom of God in a mystery, even
the hidden wisdom, which God...ordained before the
world unto our glory:

Verse 8: which none of the princes of this world knew: for
had they known it, they would not have crucified the
Lord of glory.

Verse 9: But as it is written, Eye hath not seen, nor ear heard,
neither have entered into the heart of man, the things
which God hath prepared for them that love him.

Verse 10: But God hath revealed them unto us by his Spirit:
for the Spirit searcheth all things, yea, the deep things
of God.

This passage of Matthew and Luke is important to every believer because we can see in plain view the real truth concerning the death, burial, and resurrection of Christ, but let us take a look at this picture of the Cross, the greatest story ever told.

We want to notice that nothing happens of its own; this event or this story was predestinated that Jesus the Son of God would be crucified and the two unnamed malefactors was picked by God by divine appointment to be in this place at that time to have an appointment with Jesus.

Now they led him to the place and the malefactors with Him and they crucified Him there, they lay him down on a rugged cross, they took long spikes and nailed one in his right hand, the blood starts gushing out, they took another spike and nailed it in His left hand and the blood came gushing out, they cross His feet and took a long spike and nailed His feet to that old rugged cross, and the blood came gushing out. He screamed, tears came from His eyes, and the crowd cheered.

There were three holes dug in the ground on Calvary; the hole they dug for Jesus was three feet: the first foot represented one day, the second foot represented two days, and the third foot represented three days. The crowd cheered as though it was a great festival, and they lifted Him up and put the cross down in the holes (this is by divine revelation).

St. John 12:32

> And I, if I be lifted up from the earth, will draw all
> men unto me. They also placed the malefactors, one
> on his left and one on his right.

Notation: No blood of Jesus is ever wasted just by falling to the ground. We will expound on this later.

After they lifted Him up, the blood continuously dripped to the ground; the blood meant His life was leaving Him, His body became weak. I know how weak a body feels when the blood leaves you; in 2010, the blood was running from my intestines. They took seven inches off my intestines to stop the bleeding. They carried me to ICU, and there while in ICU, I started losing blood, and my pressure started falling. My body became weaker and weaker, and the nurse said, "Somebody pray, Young's pressure is going down."

Roy Lee Goldsmith was there and my wife, Linda Young, was there; they were praying, however, the pressure kept falling. A voice whispered to me and said, "Young, pray for yourself."

I remember what the scripture had said, "When you get to the place, that you couldn't pray for yourself, the Holy Spirit would intercede and speak the words that you can't speak for yourself." My prayer was "Lord, have mercy, I am in your Hands." I felt, at this time, the breath I used to say this would be my last because my body felt weak, but all of a sudden, the pressure started rising, and the nurse said, "It still rising," and she screamed again and said, "He is stable, it's all right now."

It was not God's will that I should die. He willed me to live, but it wasn't so with Jesus; it was God's will that He die. It was for this purpose that He came into the world and died that the world through Him might be saved.

Let us take a look at this picture. Everybody that was anybody was there around Calvary: the Governor was there, Pilate was there, the Roman soldiers were there, the Jews that turned Jesus over to the soldiers were there, the centurions were there, and His followers were there, the mother of Zebedee's children was there, Mary Magdalene was there, Mary the mother of Jesus was there, the women were there standing afar off, and John the beloved Disciple was there.

Hanging between the earth and heavens, Jesus said, "Forgive them for they know not what they do." They mocked him, some wagging their heads, walking beneath the cross and saying, "Thou that destroyest the temple and build it in three days, save thyself, if thou be the son of God, come down from the cross."

John 3:16-17

Verse 16: for God so loved the world, He gave His only
begotten Son, that whosoever believed in Him should
not perish, but have everlasting life.

Verse 17: For God sent not his Son into the world to condemn
the world; but that the world through Him might be
saved.

Jesus ignores the plea from the ground because He had taught His
Disciples.

St. Mark 9:31

Verse 31: For He taught His disciples and said unto them, the
Son of man is delivered into the hands of men, and
they shall kill him; and after that he is killed, he shall
rise the third day.

Jesus ignored them, because the scripture had to be fulfilled, that He
must be put to death.

Matthew 27:40—42

Verse 40: and say thou that destroyest the temple, and buildest
it in three days, save thyself. If thou be the son of
God, come down from the cross.

Verse 41: Likewise also the chief priests mocking him, with
the scribes and elders, said,

Verse 42: He saved others, Himself he cannot save, if he be
the King of Israel, let him now come down from the
cross, and we will believe Him.

Notation: Jesus ignored them because they were unbelievers, and
the words "Come down from the cross" is a command word in this
passage. Jesus does not take His orders beside him or beneath Him.
Jesus's orders comes from above from God and He alone.

Matthew 27:49

Verse 49: Let be...that is to say let Him alone. Let's see if Elias
will come and save Him.

Luke 23:39

Verse 39: And one of the malefactors, which hanged with
Jesus, railed on him, saying if thou be the Christ saved
thyself and us, this thief represented unbelievers,
including him and them that stood on the ground.

Now, let's note that Jesus did not respond to him. He did not
respond to the unbeliever on the ground, neither did He respond to
the unbeliever on the cross. Jesus does not respond to unbelief; it is not
important when one talks to Jesus, but it's very important when Jesus
talks to you!

But the other believing thief rebuked the unbelieving thief, saying,
"Does not thou fear God, seeing thou art in the same condemnation?"
This man had a divine revelation by faith while hanging on the cross;
he saw Jesus and at the same time he saw God, for John 14:9 says, "He
that hath seen me hath seen the Father," and St. John 10:30 says, "I and
my Father are one." The reason he could see him is because his heart
was pure. Matthew 5:8 says, "Bless are the pure in heart, for they shall
see God." Also his mind was transformed and he confesses, according
to Luke 23:41-42.

And we indeed justly; for we receive the due reward of our deeds:
but this man has done nothing amiss.

Verse 42: he owns Jesus as his Lord, and he said unto Jesus,
Lord remember me when thou comest into Thy
kingdom. And Jesus said unto him, verily I say unto
thee, today, thou shalt be with me in paradise.

This man stood openly before the world owning Jesus as his Lord
and Savior. Jesus said, "If you are ashamed to own me before men, I
will be ashamed to own you before my Father." This believing man had
enough faith and enough vision while hanging on the cross; he looks
beyond the grave and see the kingdom of God and he just asks Jesus to
remember him.

It was from the six to the ninth hour when darkness covered the face of the earth. Three hours, three long hours, Jesus explains the divine revelation and the transformation of the believer that was hanging with him.

And there on Calvary, the three-foot hole that had already been dug to stand the base of Jesus's cross that was placed in, this represented three days that Jesus would disappear from the earth. Now Matthew 12:40 stated, as Jonas was three days and three nights in the whale's belly, so shall the son of man be in the heart of the earth.

Matthew 11:27 says, "All things are delivered unto me of my Father: and no man knoweth the Son, but the Father; neither knoweth any man the Father, save the Son, and he to whomsoever the Son will reveal him. So Jesus chooses to reveal himself and the Father to the believing malefactor, we want to note that when he went to Calvary, he was lost, but he was a lost sheep. When he went to the cross, he was condemned, he was a condemned sheep, when he went to the cross, he was a sinner, but he was a sheep, God cleanse him, God forgives him, and Jesus saves him, he now is no longer a sinner, but he is saved by faith through grace while hanging on the cross."

In Luke 19:10, Jesus said, "I come to seek and to save that which 'was' lost," so the thief is now saved because Jesus used the word "was lost," and he find that which was lost, at Calvary hanging on the cross. This is a symbolic picture of what Jesus was talking about in Luke 15 about the man leaving a hundred sheep and going to look for that one which was lost and heaven rejoices over one lost sheep that comes to repentance. I see the angels right now rejoicing in heaven over this lost sinner that has come to repentance.

One of our great Hymn penned by the great John Newton, "Amazing Grace, how sweet the sound, that save a wretch like me, I once was lost, but now I am found, was blind, but now I see. Twas grace that taught my heart to fear, and grace my fears relieved, how precious did that grace appeared, the hour I first believe!"

This malefactor that had this divine revelation was never the same, as he was before he went to Calvary, because no man can't look into the perfect will of God and see the power and glory of God and be the same; it's like looking into a mirror: you can't see Jesus without seeing yourself. When you see Jesus and His righteousness and how perfect He is, a man can only see his imperfection and his weakness.

The veil of the temple was rent in twain, from the top to the bottom, and the earth did quake and the rocks rent and the graves was open and many bodies of the saints which slept rose. Let us note there was an earthquake, the temple had burst from top to bottom, and the rocks was broke and graves were open, the dead rose or came to life, but they didn't come out of the grave until three days later because Jesus had to be the first one to put His foot on Resurrection ground because the scripture declared that he was the first fruit. And the earth busted also; when the earth busted, the water table below the earth was exposed. The blood that had dropped from Jesus's hands, head, and feet to the earth fell to the water tables.

First, this great revelation tells us that the dirt represented man; that's where he came from. God created man from the dust of the earth, and it was the shedding of Jesus's blood that saved him.

Observation

The rulers and all officials saw only the events: they saw the veil break in pieces, they heard the sounds, and the rock busted and the earth quake and saw Jesus cry and die. They saw it get dark, but the centurion saw the transformation of the sinner, the power and the glory of God; he began shouting, praising, and glorifying God, so there was one hanging on the cross that saw the power and the glory of God, and with these two witnesses, a fact was established that God is real! God is real! God is real!

And when he saw him meant some time had passed; he didn't see this in the beginning, but just a glimpse, but he kept listening and looking until he saw him, the Lord of lords and King of kings. It does not matter how long it takes, just keep on waiting and watching; if you seek you will find; if you ask, it shall be given; if you knock, the door will be open unto you.

Was he saved? Yes, absolutely, after having a divine revelation, after being washed with the blood of Jesus, after seeing the kingdom, certainly he was saved. The centurion not only saw the power and glory of God, but saw the righteousness of Jesus, and his testimony was "Surely this was a righteous man."

St. John 19:31—36

Verse 31: The Jews therefore, because it was the preparation, that the bodies should not remain upon the cross on the Sabbath day, (for the Sabbath day was a high day), besought Pilate that their legs might be broken, and that they might be taken away.

Verse 32: Then came the soldiers, and break the legs of the first, and of the other which was crucified with him.

Let us note that they break the legs of the unbelieving thief first, because it didn't matter what time he died, but

it did matter when the believing thief died, they had
not yet pierced Jesus in the side.

Verse 33: but when they came to Jesus, and saw that he was
dead already, they break not his legs:

Verse 34: bur one of the soldiers pierced his side with a spear,
and immediately blood and water came out.

By God's divine power, some of the blood from Jesus's side gushed on the believer before he took his last breath. Jesus's blood cleansed him and redeemed him before he died. Now it has been discussed, argued, debated down through the centuries by scholars, laypeople, theologians on whether the thief was baptized. I submit by divine insight that when Jesus was pierced in his side, the blood and water gushed out onto the believing man, and he received the blood and the water directly from the savior's side. Remember that the blood from his hand, head, and feet that was on the ground when the ground busted went first to the water tables; the rest of the blood, after Jesus was pierce in the side, washed the believer, and the rest went to the water tables. And God troubled the water and commanded the pressure of the water by His divine power pushes his blood throughout the world all the way back to first man, Adam. Everything that comes from God must go back to God!

Now let's note the believing malefactor did nothing at all to be saved; Jesus did it all. In the final analysis, it will not matter at the end what kind of rituals are practiced or what kind of worship services we may have, everything we do today is only symbolic of what happened on Calvary. Salvation is not by works or anything man can do that secure salvation, it's by faith and faith alone that saves.

St John 19:35, 'And he that saw it bare record, and his record is true, and he knoweth it that he saith truth, that ye might believe."

We want to explore the saying of Jesus, "Today thou shalt be with me in Paradise."

Jesus speaks in this passage about everything that was to happen beyond the grave. He tells this to the malefactor who believed, and the malefactor believed Him, then Jesus lets him see it, and when he saw it, he said, "Lord, remember me when thou come in, not if you come in." Everybody around the cross use the word "if" but you would note the malefactor said, "When you come into thy kingdom," he had no doubt, no doubt at all about his salvation.

This preacher that write these things is declaring that this believing malefactor went to the cross as nothing, wretch and undone, condemned and filthy, but found righteousness at the cross.

When I think about what happened on the cross and I think about my own salvation, it leaves me to share this great hymn, "At the Cross!"

Alas and did my savior bleed, and did my sovereign die, would he devote that sacred head for such a worm as I, at the cross, at the cross, where I first saw the light, and the burdens of my heart rolled away, it was there by faith, I received my sight, and now I am happy all the day!

What is Paradise? Paradise is a spirit world, the soul of man when he dies goes back to God, the body goes in the grave, and the spirit goes to the spirit world; that's called Paradise.

Where is Paradise? Paradise is in the heart of the earth, Matthew 12:40, which is also the lower part of the earth.

Where did Jesus go after death to fulfill the promise to the thief when he replied, "Thou shalt be with me in Paradise"? There are those that said he went to heaven and took the thief with him. This is not so; here is the truth about this matter, found in 1 Peter 3:18-19, "For Christ has also once suffered for sin, the just for the unjust that He might bring us to God. Being put to death in the flesh, but quicken by the spirit; by which also he went and preached unto the spirits in prison, which sometimes were disobedient when once the long suffering of God waited in the days of Noah."

Christ went to this place called Paradise, by the spirit according to the scripture; they put His body in the grave, and according to the scripture, He preached three days and three nights in the heart of the earth. Now what did He preach? You noticed that Jesus had already died on the Cross; the malefactor was still alive when Jesus got to

Paradise. He couldn't take His text until the thief got there because He had promised him he would be with Him in Paradise, so when Jesus took His text, the malefactor was standing by His side.

Now the first day, His text was creation and the law. He talked about how the world was formed and how His Father had made everything, and He talked about how God had made provision for Him in the Garden of Eden, and God had given Him everything that He needed to live, of every seed, every tree for meat, and then God issued His first commandment handed down to man, "Thou shalt eat of all the trees in the garden, but there is one tree in the midst of the garden thou shalt not eat thereof, the day that you eat of this tree, you shall surely die."

Jesus kept preaching, and he tells them about the fall of man. He tells them He took a rib out of Adam's side and made him a helpmeet, her name was Eve, mother of all the living; she strolled in the garden one day, and there she met Satan in the form of a serpent, and he convinced her to eat the fruit thereof. She took it, she ate it and gave some to her husband, Adam. It was right there, man that God had made disobeyed the only commandment; right there the sentence that God had promised man, the day he eat of the fruit, was carried out. That day man lost his connection with God; he lost his favor with God. God came walking in the cool of the day to bring judgment on man. God asked Adam, "What had thou done, did you eat of the fruit I told you not to?"

He said, "It was the woman," then God asked the woman, "What is this thou hast done?" She said, "It was the snake, he beguiled me and I did eat and I gave it to my husband." And the Lord God said unto the serpent, "Because thou hast done this, thou art cursed above all cattle, and above every beast of the field; upon thou belly shalt thou go, and dust shalt thou eat all the days of thy life." Unto the woman, He said, "I will greatly multiply thy sorrow and conception; in sorrow thou shalt bring forth children; and thou desires shall be to thy husband, and he shall rule over thee." And unto Adam He said, "Because thou hast hearken unto the voice of thy wife, and has eaten of the tree, of which I commanded thee, saying thou shalt not eat it: curse is the ground for thy sake: and sorrow shalt thou eat of it all the days of thy life: thorns also and thistles shall it bring forth to thee, and thou shalt eat the herbs of the field: in the sweat of thy face shalt thou eat bread, till though return unto the ground: for out of it wast thou taken: for dust thou art, and unto dust shalt thou return." God drove them both out of the garden, for this cause all of you are here in captivity, it is because of sin that put him here, and it is sin that has put you here.

Jesus presses on in His sermon with power and authority, and He talked about the lawlessness, and He preached about Moses and the law, how that he sent ten commandments and all of them were broken, and you couldn't keep them because you were weak in the flesh, and the breaking of my laws brought all of you to this place, condemned and in captivity.

The Second Day. His text was grace. He talks about favor of God, that which is obtained without works, and He explains how in their day how sins were atoned by burnt offerings and sacrifices, and He preached to them that the ram and bullocks and goats was only to cover man's sin, but the sin remained, and every time a man sinned, he had to bring an offering to the priest to cover that particular sin. Jesus presses on in His sermon, and He tells them how they would take two birds, kill one bird and cut into two, and dip the other bird in the blood and set the other free, one died and one was set free. And many, many other things that Jesus told them; in the final analysis, He preached a more excellent way and that way was, not covering their sins, but to take their sins away. For this purpose, Jesus died on the Cross that the world through Him might be saved, and my Father sent me to this place to save all of you, and I shed my blood that I might redeem you back to God and the fellowship with which I now stand.

The Third Day. Jesus preached Faith, and He started with God so loved the world that He gave His only begotten Son, that whosoever believed in Him, shall not perish, but shall have everlasting life. He preaches, He continues to preach that faith was the substance of things hoped for and the evidence of things not seen. And then He answer an age-old question that Job had asked centuries early, if a man die, can he live again? Jesus stands and gives Job his answer, and Jesus answers that question, that I am the resurrection and the life, and he that believeth in me, though he be dead, yet shall he live, and he that liveth and believeth in me shall never die. Oh, this must have made Job happy, this gave him hope and everyone else there hope and made them happy. Jesus presses on in His sermon; he that believeth in me, have life, and he that does not believeth in me hast not life, come unto me, all ye that labor and are heavy laden, and I will give thee rest. He tells them to believe in Him, He tells them to trust in Him, and He tells them that I am the way, the truth, and the life, any man cometh unto me, shall find rest and peace for his soul. Here Jesus opens the doors of the New Testament church (Notation), Peter opens the first church Above, and Jesus opens up the first church Beyond.

All of what Jesus said and done, these three days cannot be written in this book.

Jesus holds three keys in His hands: one key was to hell, one key was to death, and one key to the kingdom. He takes the keys to death and hell and unlocks the door, and He takes the keys to the kingdom and open up Himself, and He said, "I am the door, by me if any man enter in, he shall be saved. He swings the doors of prison open, He being the door." The believer that hanged on the cross with Him stands with Him, as Jesus said, "Whosoever will let him come," and the believing saint ushered everybody in that came through the door of Jesus Christ.

When they came out into His kingdom, He gave them gifts. He took captivity that had held them captive and led captivity away, and then, He gave gifts unto men. He gave them the gifts of Grace and mercy, the gift of faith, and the gift of the Holy Ghost because Jesus knew that this same spirit that He gave unto them, that will raise Him from the dead, will also raise them in the last day immortal with a glorified body like unto His. Then He gave the benediction as the New Testament church in the lower part of the earth, in the Spirit world, and since He was the end of the law, and the prophets, the law having no power, the prophets having no power, Jesus makes ready to come back through the grave, leaving the believing thief that hanged with him in charge, giving him power and authority to preach the gospel throughout the spirit world.

Now Jesus takes the other two keys: death and hell, unlocks the graves, and He takes the sting from death and said, "O death where is thou sting," and He said to the grave, "O grave where is thou victory," and stands upon resurrection ground and said, "All power has been given unto me in heaven and in earth," and He walks through the streets of Jerusalem with saints of old that followed Him, the saints being seen by those in the city; this was a testimony that they did rise, this was the first resurrection.

What happened to them? By faith, Enoch was translated, and when they searched for him, he could not be found. Because God had translated him, this is what happened to the saints that were resurrected from the dead; Jesus, having all power in His Hands, translated them to another dimension with the same power that God translated Enoch. With man, this is impossible, but with God all things are possible. God is the same yesterday, today, forever; in the beginning, God created the heaven and the earth, the world, and everything therein in six days, that is in heaven above and the earth beneath.

After translating them, Jesus remained on the earth some forty days. You see, God made worlds, Jesus worked in those worlds, and he spoke in those places. Scientists desire to find them and life. There is life, but it's not human life, it's supernatural life. How did Jesus go there? For example, there used to be a television show that starred Mr. Spock and Captain Kirk, and they could beam Mr. Spock from one planet to another' this is human mind, Jesus being supernatural could move through time and space from one dimension to another just by thought. If he stands in the Holy city and thinks New York, he would be there that fast and appear in that body; he could walk in a room with windows and doors shut and appear because that body is not fashion of this world.

He that Hath an ear let him hear, He that Hath an eye, let him see!

The great Andrea Crouch wrote in 1962, "The Blood of Jesus Will Never Lose Its Power"

The blood that Jesus shed for me

Way back on Calvary

The blood that gives me strength

From day to day

It will never lose its power
It reaches to the highest mountain
It flows to the lowest valley
The blood that gives me strength
From day to day
It will never lose its power

ABOUT THE AUTHOR
REV. DR. RICHARD E. YOUNG

I have never told this story before, the reason being, because at the time, there was unbelief, so I said I wouldn't tell anyone. Some forty (40) years later I have decided to tell this story so some will know that Christ is alive and real.

On a Thursday night in 1969, there appeared the risen Christ while I was at work in my office, the risen Christ stood behind me, his presence changed the whole room and took all of the strength out of my body, I was 22 years of age at the time, I had been praying and fasting, because I wanted to see Him. All I had to do was turn around and I would have seen Him, but I felt like I was going to die, I didn't know if He was going to lay his right hand on me, fearing that I would die, I didn't turn around, and I said, 'now Lord', now Lord', now Lord', the third time I utter these words, immediately the 'strength returned into my body. I rose from my seat praising God!

There was a day after the resurrection had passed, he was seen by 500 brethren at one time, then he was seen of the twelve where they were assembled, the scripture said, God has no respect of person, it was my faith, that if others have seen Him, I could to, I had no doubt in mind that I would see Him someday, and from that day I have been glorifying God!!

Dr. Young has deep studies in the Old and New Testament Doctrine, Systematic Theology, Studies in Religion and Expository Preaching, however, none of these studies are related to what's written in this book. This entire book was given by divine revelation and the honor must go to God Almighty. I am humbled that he chose me to reveal this great mystery that the world is hungry for.